THE ESSENTIAL RUMI QUOTES

TOP 300
MOST INSPIRING

BY
RUMI NETWORK

Rumi Network
www.Rumi.net

PUBLICATION
Title: The Essential Rumi Quotes
Subtitle: Top 300 Most Inspiring
Compiled and Published by: Rumi Network
ISBN: 9798871290651
Publication Date: December 2023
Number of Pages: 164
© Copyright Valentino St. Germain (Shahram Shiva)
All Rights Reserved.

WEBSITE
www.Rumi.net

CONTACT, RIGHTS REQUEST
contact@rumi.net

TOPICS

PREFACE

The Western civilization has always been mesmerized by Eastern thought, philosophy, rituals and culture. The most prominent examples are the teachings and stories from the Old and the New Testaments. Fables from the adventures of Sinbad and One Thousand and One Nights. The ever-popular Yoga and the religious schools of Hinduism and Buddhism. Eastern occultism. Added to the list are the ancient Sumerian, Babylonian and Egyptian mystery schools.

Rumi, however, is not the first classical Persian poet to gain popularity in the West. About a hundred years ago another Persian cultural and scientific giant, Omar Khayyam, became wildly popular here. His short poems, known as quatrains or *rubaiyat*, with their tales of unabashed passion, wine drinking, partying and in short enjoying life without the burden of religious guilt became the forbidden fruit that Western readers flocked to.

Omar Khayyam, in height of his popularity in the West, was much more known than today's Rumi. For example, Khayyam is being quoted in at least four major studio Hollywood movies of the 1940s, '50s and '60s: The Music Man (1962), Payton Place (1957), Pandora and The Flying Dutchman (1951) and The Picture of Dorian Gray (1945). There is also a biopic "Omar Khayyam" (Paramount – 1957). These movies represent the very popular aspect of American culture. In contrast, except for an episode of the HBO series Six Feet Under, Rumi references are basically non-existent in American film.

I have been exploring and sharing Rumi with the world for more than 30 years. I began translating Rumi quite extemporaneously, like it was an old habit, in New York City when I was in my early 20's. The Rumi we love today is a product of the last 25 years of his life. During that period came an outpouring of many thousands of incredibly concise and thoughtful poems on varied topics. This immense artistic period occurred after the honor killing of his mentor Shams by Rumi's youngest son. Please refer to my book Rumi's Untold Story: From 30-Year Research to discover Rumi's very colorful hidden life.

Rumi's many thousands of poems cover practically every possible theme. These themes include, deeply philosophical and mystical, drunken revelries, anti-religious and anti-authoritarian outbursts, light-hearted historical tales, simple life teachings, passionate love stories and even pornographic examples. He was so prolific and adapt at creating verse that he was able to speak poetry at will.

The Essential Rumi Quotes
The Essential Rumi Quotes, offers the reader a collection of the most powerful, passionate, endearing, and inspiring quotes of Rumi, selected from my decades-long love affair with Rumi's work. I have categorized them in four sections: 1. The Power of Love; 2. Beauty, Music & Dance; 3. Hope,

Recovery & Death; 4. The Ascended Master, The Teachings.

THE POWER OF LOVE

The first selection is his wildly popular passionate love quotes. Rumi views love as the real vehicle for growth. However, he teaches that the experience and manifestation of love begins and ends with you. As Rumi points out in many of his poems (where these quotes have been selected), toward the end of his search he learned that he was seeking himself all along and the Beloved is none other than himself. He wrote that he was knocking on the door of ascension from the inside and the true Beloved is your higher self.

BEAUTY, MUSIC & DANCE

Through his mentorship with the mystic Shams, Rumi was transformed from that of a sober scholar to an impassioned lover of music and whirling. After his transformation, all night parties with music, movement, whirling and poetry recitations became the norm.

HOPE, RECOVERY & DEATH

One of the key reasons that Rumi's work resonates with us, is due to his unrestrained and uncensored expressions of various aspects of personal and spiritual growth. His quotes on healing, hope and death have helped countless people to cope with suffering and recovery.

THE ASCENDED MASTER

This section reveals Rumi's quotes as an ascended master attacking all forms of mind and spirit oppression. Rumi reminds us over and over again that real spiritual mastery is not achieved through dogmatic thinking or conventional religions and isms. What you wear, eat or drink or your facial hair have no relevancy to growth. Only a high conformist would fantasize that wearing a certain style of dress might cause soul growth. Also, his many so-called blasphemous poems represent an evolved soul that is totally free from the shackles of hypocrisy and oppression that exist in all religious doctrines.

RELEVANT IN MORE THAN ONE GENRE
A few of the quotes would naturally be relevant in more than one genre, hence they are shared. Also, a select number of the quotes can be expressed in different ways, so these variations are also included.

It is a privilege and pleasure to share my most favorite quotes of Rumi with you.

Val St. Germain
Founder
Rumi Network

THE ESSENTIAL
RUMI QUOTES

SELECTION ONE

THE POWER OF LOVE
PASSIONATE QUOTES

This is the most popular category of Rumi's poetry. Rumi views love as the real vehicle for growth. However, he teaches that the experience and manifestation of love begins and ends with you. As Rumi points out in many of his poems, toward the end of his search he learned that he was seeking himself all along and the Beloved is nonother than himself. He wrote that he was knocking on the door of ascension from the inside and the true Beloved is your higher self.

Don't fear love.

When what you really love
beckons you, let go and let
the waves of desire take you
there. Your instincts
are you guide.

In your light, I know love. In your beauty, I make poetry. You suddenly dance inside my chest, hidden from view. My art becomes this expression.

Laugh as much as you breathe. Love as long as you live.

Love, you are my certainty. Lift me to the stars. This "I" is a figment of my imagination.

The one who was always in my thoughts, for whom I've searched so long, has come to me with open arms, laying flowers on my path.

Be warmed with love, for only love exists. Where is intimacy except in giving and receiving.

When lovers of life get ready to dance, the earth shakes and the sky trembles.

How can you ever hope to
know the Beloved without
becoming in every cell the
lover?

Love is the bridge
between you and
everything.

A life without Love
isn't a life.

First there is the calamity
of love. When the lover
has lost his senses and his
bearings, then the teacher
appears.

Love is from the infinite,
and will remain until
eternity. The seeker of
love escapes the chains of
birth and death.

Your love lifts my soul
from the body to the sky,
and you lift me up out of
the two worlds.

We have become one in such a way, that I am confused whether I am you, or you are me.

Caught by our own thoughts, we worry about everything, but once we get drunk on that love, whatever will be, will be.

A true lover doesn't follow
any one religion,
be sure of that.

Love is best when mixed
with anguish. In our town,
we won't call you a lover
if you escape the pain.

Tonight is the night.
It's the creation of that
land of eternity.
It's not an ordinary night,
it's a wedding of those
who seek love.

To deal with you hiding
behind your holiness, I
seek a good time instead.

I am powerless by love's game. How can you expect me to behave and act modest?

Die in love and stay alive forever.

Love came and moved
like blood in my body. It
rushed through my veins
and encircled my heart.

Love is the strand that
connects you to you.

If your heart is not with me, sitting together is not enough.

The lover and the Beloved are like a mirror for each other, one is the cause for the other's effect.

A true lover doesn't follow
any one religion, since in
the religion of love, there
is no church or priest.

I've become a rose petal
and you are like the wind
for me, take me for a ride.

They say love opens a
door from one heart to
another. But if there is no
wall, how can there be a
door.

If I love myself, I love
you. If I love you,
I love myself.

The minute I heard my
first love story, I started
looking for you.

True lovers aren't formed
by chance. They are for
each other from the start.

There is a path from me to you that I am constantly searching for.

A true lover doesn't follow any one religion, since in the religion of love, there is no irreverence or faith.

Love elevates you to
the next level.

You are the comfort of my
soul. You are the wealth
of my spirit.

Find the sweetness in your own heart, then you may find the sweetness in every heart.

I am yours. Don't give me back to myself again.

Your heart and my heart
are very old friends.

Love is not an emotion; it
is your very existence.

I don't want learning, or dignity, or respectability. I want this music, and this dawn, and the warmth of your cheek against mine.

When you seek love with all your heart, you'll find that its cchocs throughout the universe.

I want that love that will
raise the dead.

I want that love that brings
out the beauty of silence.

Choose love.
Choose love.

It is the inner bond that
draws one person to
another, not words.

You may learn by reading,
but you will understand
with love.

The love you seek with all
your heart, echoes
throughout the universe.

Every moment is made
glorious by the light of
love.

The message behind the
words is the voice
of the heart.

Remember, love is reckless, but reason pursues a profit. True love is all-consuming and totally unabashed.

A lifetime without love is of no account.

Love is the Water of Life.

Beloved, am I the seeker
or the sought? Until I am
I, you are another. There
is no place for "You" and
"I".

Your task is not to seek
love, but to search and
find all the barriers within
yourself that you have
built against it.

Love knows the way.

Let's delight in one
another, before there is no
more of you and I.

Let's get drunk on one
another, before there is no
more of you and I.

Ask from yourself for
yourself. All the universe
is already within you.
Love is the whole thing.

Silence is the
language of love.

I don't want learning. I want the warmth of your cheek against mine.

The music brightens the house of lovers.

Love said to me, there is
nothing that is not me.
Be silent.

Lovers find secret places
inside this violent world.

In love, aside from sipping
the wine of timelessness,
nothing else exists.

I said, First I know you,
then I die. He said, For the
one who knows me, there
is no dying.

You reap what you sow, if you have any sense my friend, don't plant anything but love.

Lose your soul in love, I swear, there is no other way.

Let the fire of love burn my sorrow and purify my soul, so I can fly without wings.

Open your arms, if you want to be held.

Love comes to you of its own accord, and the yearning for it cannot be learned in any school.

Goodbyes are only for those who love with their eyes. For those who love with their heart and soul there is no such thing as separation.

They say there is a
doorway from heart to
heart but what is the use of
a door when there are no
walls?

I once had a thousand
desires, but in my one
desire to know you, all
others melted away.

I want to know the joy of
you whisper "more".

The minute I heard my
first love story, I started
looking for you, not
knowing, how blind that
was.

Lovers don't finally meet
somewhere, they're in
each other all along.

I want that love that is the
silence of eternity.

Why struggle to open the
door between you and I,
when the separation is
an illusion.

Laugh as much as you
breathe. Love as long as
you live.

You reap what you sow.
With life as short as a
breath, don't plant
anything but love.

Why should I seek?
I'm the same as he. His
essence speaks through
me. I've been looking
for myself.

Your face lights up like a
flower in bloom when hit
with the truth of love.

If you want the moon, do
not hide at night. If you
want a rose, do not hide
from thorns. If you want
love, do not hide from
yourself.

Love is best when mixed
with anguish.
In our town, we won't
call you a Lover
if you escape the pain.

Look for Love in this way,
welcome it to your soul,
and watch your spirit fly
away in ecstasy.

You think you are alive
because you breathe air?
Shame on you,
that you are alive in such a
limited way.
Don't be without Love,
so you won't feel dead.
Die in Love
and stay alive forever.

I am a patient of Love,
and you are like
medicine for me.

Every cell,
taking wings,
flies about the world.
All seek separately
the many faces of my
love.

We have become one
in such a way,
That I am confused
whether
I am you,
or you are me.

This world is no match for
your Love.

The path of Love,
has seventy-two folds
and countless facets.
Your love and religion
is all about control,
deceit and hypocrisy,
you go back to sleep.

Without wings, without
feathers, I fly about
looking for you.
I have become a rose
petal and you are like
the wind for me.
Take me for a ride.

If I pray it's only so my
heart would turn toward
you.

SELECTION TWO

BEAUTY, MUSIC & DANCE
CELEBRATION OF THE ARTS

Through his mentorship with the mystic Shams, Rumi was transformed from that of a sober scholar to an impassioned lover of music and whirling. After his transformation, all night parties with music, movement, whirling and poetry recitations became the norm.

If they ask what you do,
say I create beauty in
all things.

I have come to bring out
the beauty you never knew
you had and lift you up
like a prayer to the sky.

Dance as you rise above
the two worlds. Dance to
tear your heart to pieces
and give up your soul.

When you dance the
whole universe dances.

I have come to bring out
the beauty in you.

When you finally see your
own true beauty, you will
become an idol for
yourself.

I want that love that brings
out the beauty of silence.

Unfold your
own myth.

Dance, when you're broken open. Dance and become free.

Beauty surrounds us.

A bird doesn't care who
hears it sing. Be like that.

One morning, a presence
comes over your soul.
You heart sings. You
begin to dance.

You are not meant for crawling. Use your golden wings and fly.

Dance as you rise above the two worlds. Dance as if to burst your heart and give up your soul.

Dance like
no one is watching.

Inside you there's an artist
you don't know about.

You were born with
wings.

Let the beauty we love
be what we do.

When I am silent, I fall
into the place where
everything is music.

Dancing is not getting up
randomly like a speck of
dust blown around in the
wind.

Of those who are blind to
your beauty and deaf to
your songs, why do you
worry?

The only lasting beauty is
the truth of the heart.

The ground's generosity takes in our compost and grows beauty! Try to be more like the ground.

Be silent, and go into that place where everything is music.

SELECTION THREE

HOPE, RECOVERY
& DEATH
HEALING QUOTES

One of the key reasons that Rumi's work resonates with us, is due to his unrestrained and uncensored expressions of various aspects of personal and spiritual growth. His quotes on healing, hope and death have helped countless people to cope with suffering and recovery.

Come, come, whoever you are, a pagan, an idol worshiper or an infidel. Come, even if you have broken your vows a thousand times. Ours is not a caravan of despair. Come.

Let go of your cup filled with yesterday, instead drink the nectar of this moment.

Your defects are the ways
that glory gets manifested.

Don't give me back to my
old companions. Inside
you my yearning stops.

It is your turn now. You
waited; you were patient.
The time has come for us
to polish you. We will
transform your inner pearl
into a house of fire.

Oh, soul,
you worry too much.

He smiled like a rose in
full bloom, he said, come
into the heart of fire.
There you will see what
you thought was a flame,
is only jasmine.

Don't act so small, you
have the whole universe
inside you.

Sorrow said to me, all this joy that you have brought to the world has killed my business completely.

Your body is like a guest house, receiving company from the hidden world. Some are positive, some are tragic and still others who are frantic.

Try not to resist the changes that come your way. Instead, let life flow through you.

Do not worry that your life is turning upside down. Welcome change.

When were you ever
made less by dying?

Giving thanks for
abundance is greater than
the abundance itself.

The wound is where the
light enters you.

Any pain you may feel, is
a messenger, listen to it.

Don't search among the
branches when the answer
is in the roots.

If you find every stroke of
your soul irritating, how
will you ever be polished.

Don't grieve.
Anything lost, returns
in another form.

You're almost there, just
follow my guide.

If everything around
seems dark, you may need
to brighten your own light.

Ignore all who wish to
dim your light.

Don't resist the uplifting
changes that come
your way.

How much light can you
hold inside you? Expand
your horizons and let
more light in.

The one who points the
finger is to blame.

Everything is choice.
Choose joy,
not pain or sorrow.

Birds earn their
wings by falling.

Keep walking.
Keep moving forward.
Keep pushing through.

Never give from the
depths of your well,
protect your core.

Don't bother explaining to
those who don't resonate.
People are closed
to the truth.

Learn the alchemy of soul
evolution in human form.
The moment you
understand what growth
really is, the
door will open.

Empower yourself and
you'll grow greater than
the world. Only then your
true self will be
revealed to you

The sum of my whole life
is in these three sayings:
I was raw. I got cooked.
I was freed.

Half of life is lost in
charming others. The
other half is lost in going
through anxieties caused
by others. Rise above this
cruel game.

Being a candle is not easy,
in order to give light,
one must first burn.

Life is a balance between
holding on and letting go.

You are not meant for
crawling. Use your golden
wings and fly.

Gratitude is like wine for
the soul. Go and have
your fill.

I said: What about my heart? He said: What you hold inside it? I said: Pain and sorrow. He said: The wound is the place where the light enters you.

There is a void in your soul, ready to be filled.

Don't feel lonely. The entire universe is inside you.

The ground's generosity takes in our compost and grows beauty. Try to be more like the ground.

Death has nothing to do
with going away. The sun
sets. The moon sets.
But they are not gone.

Don't grieve.
Anything you lose comes
around in another form.

Every mortal will taste
death, but only some
will taste life.

Before death takes away
what you are given, give
away what there is to give.

Knock and the door will open. Vanish and you shine like the sun. Fall and you will rise to the heavens. Become nothing, and you will become everything.

Be like a tree, let the dead leaves drop.

No one is actually dead
until the ripples they cause
in the world fade away.

In the blackest of your
moments, wait with no
fear.

You have to keep breaking
your heart, until it opens.

I died a mineral and came
back a plant. I died a plant
and rose an animal. I died
an animal and I was man.
Why should I fear? When
have I ever been
less by dying?

The hurt you embrace
becomes joy.

Anything you lose comes
around in another form.

Suffering is a gift -
in it is hidden mercy.

The moment you admit
the troubles you've been
given; a door will open.

Our death is our wedding
with eternity.

Darkness can also be your
candle. You must brave
through shadow and light.

Leave this world like the
essence of rose that
passes through the
perfumer's still.

Your shadow self
has been serving you.

SELECTION FOUR

THE ASCENDED MASTER
LIFE AND SPIRITUAL TEACHINGS

Rumi's reminds us over and over again that real spiritual mastery is not achieved through dogmatic thinking or conventional teachings found in religion and isms. What you wear, eat or drink, or your facial hair for that matter, have no relevancy to spiritual growth. Only a high conformist would fantasize that wearing a certain style of dress might cause soul growth. Also, his many so-called blasphemous quotes represent an evolved soul that is totally free from the shackles of hypocrisy and oppression that exist in all religious doctrines.

Come, come, whoever you are, a pagan, an idol worshiper or an infidel. Come, even if you have broken your vows a thousand times. Ours is not a caravan of despair. Come.

Lie down with your eyes closed, watch the sky bloom with hundreds of bright, sparkling flowers.

Set your life on fire.
Seek those who fan
your flames.

If light is in your heart,
you will find your
way home.

Be silent, and go into
that place where
everything is music.

Go find yourself first, so
you can also find me.

The middle path is the
way to wisdom.

There is a morning inside
you waiting to
burst into light.

Stop acting so small. You
are the universe in
ecstatic motion.

The desire to know your
own soul will end
all other desires.

When you surpass the human state, your angelic nature will unfold beyond this world. Surpass event the angels then enter that timeless ocean.

What matters is how quickly you do what your soul wants.

Observe the wonders
around you. Feel the
artistry moving through
and be silent.

On this path let the heart
be your guide.

The very center of your
heart is where life begins.
The most beautiful
place on earth.

Respond to every call that
ignites your spirit.

It's your road and yours
alone. Others may walk it
with you, but no one can
walk it for you.

You're a gold mine.
Did you know that, hidden
in the dust of the earth.
It is your turn now, to be
placed in fire. Let us
cremate your impurities.

The infidels aren't lost.
You are lost. That's why
everyone else seems
lost to you.

This world is teeming with
the presence of Christ.

Stop thinking small.
You have the whole
universe inside you.

Everything that you seek.
You are already that.

Do you know what you are? You are a manuscript of a divine letter. You are a mirror reflecting a noble face.

This universe is not outside of you.
Look inside yourself.
Everything that you seek, you are already that.

Show me an intellect gone
mad and I will show you a
soul departed for good.

I have lost myself in God,
and now God is mine.
Don't look for Him in
every direction, for
He is in my soul.

In the path of union, the wise man and the mad man are one.

What you are seeking is also seeking you.

Your heart knows the
way. Run in that direction.

The "infidels" aren't lost.
You are lost, that is why
everyone else seems lost.

Yesterday I was clever, so
I wanted to change the
world. Today I am wise, I
am changing myself.

Only from the heart can
you touch the sky.
In the path of union, the
wise man and the mad
man are one.

What a Joy, to travel the
way of the heart.

You are not a drop in the
ocean. You are the entire
ocean in a drop.

Why should I seek? I'm
the same as he.
His essence speaks
through me. I've been
looking for myself.

There is a voice that
doesn't use words, listen.

Sell your cleverness and
buy bewilderment.

You are the drop
and the ocean.

The words you speak
become the house
you live in.

Little by little, you will
turn into a whole sweet
amorous universe.

You've seen my descent.
Now watch my rising.

Of those who are blind to
your beauty and deaf to
your songs, why do you
worry?

Build a ship, and there
will be water to greet it.

Why are you so enchanted
by this world, when a
mine of gold lies
within you?

When the oceans surge let
them splash inside
your chest.

There is an unseen
presence that
bestows gifts.

When will you begin that
long journey into
yourself?

Like melting snow, wash
yourself of yourself.

We hold inside the wonders we seek outside.

Don't search among the branches when the answer is in the roots.

There is a voice that doesn't use words. Listen!

You were born with wings, why crawl through life.

Unfold your own myth.

My soul is from
elsewhere; I know I will
end up there.

Don't place kisses on my
tombstone after I die,
smother me with
them now.

Everything holds a
pleasing form, but not
everyone appreciates it.

What you seek,
is seeking you.

May your instincts be
your guide.

Welcome,
now be fearless.

My words are fire.

You are the truth from
head to toe.

As you start to walk,
the way appears.

You send out blessings
like blossoms falling
around you.

Joy is closer to the truth
than pain or sorrow.
Choose joy.

The water also seeks
the thirsty.

I searched for God and
found only myself. I
searched for myself and
found only God.

It is silent that draws one
person to another,
not words.

With my mouth closed,
I spoke to you in a
hundred silent ways.

I am fierce and tender.
Fierce to those who wish
to limit me, tender to those
who wish me growth.

People who repress
desires are hypocrites.

Ignore all who wish to
dim your light.

Be shameless, if you want
to learn our secrets.

Patience is foreseeing.

Walk out of your house
like a prophet that you
know you are.

Be determined like Noah.
Build the boat, even if
the whole town laughs.

I am and I am not.
Not unlike a shadow.

Joy is hidden,
beneath sorrow.

If you could rise above
yourself for a moment, the
secret of secrets will be
revealed to you.

Learn the alchemy of the
soul evolution in human
form. The moment you
understand what growth
really is, the door
will open.

Empower yourself and
you'll grow greater than
the world. Only then your
true self will be
revealed to you.

The sum of my whole life
is in these three sayings:
I was raw. I got cooked.
I was freed.

Half of life is lost in
charming others. The
other half is lost in going
through anxieties caused
by others. Rise above this
cruel game.

Let silence be the art you
practice. The quieter you
become, the more
you hear.

As you start to walk on the
path, the way appears.

I am not the body; I am
the soul that lives within.

You are not meant for
crawling. Use your golden
wings and fly.

Gratitude is like wine for the soul. Go and have your fill.

You must ask for what you really want. Don't go back to sleep.

Yearning!

There is a void in your
soul, ready to be filled.

Inside you there's an artist
you don't yet know about.

Don't you know, it is your
light that lights the world.

Raise your words not voice, it is rain that grows flowers, not thunder.

I am in a boat made of myself by myself. I'm already under and living with the ocean.

The ground's generosity takes in our compost and grows beauty! Try to be more like the ground.

I said: What about my heart? He said: Tell me what you hold inside?

I said: What about my passion? He said: Keep it burning.

I am merely a guest, born in this world to know the secrets that lie beyond it.

Knock and the door will open. Vanish and you will shine like the sun. Fall and you will rise to the heavens. Become nothing and you will turn into everything.

Your shadow self has been serving you.

When have I been less by
dying?

I died a mineral and came
back a plant. I died a plant
and rose an animal. I died
an animal and I was a
man. Why should I
fear death?

Listen and lay your head
under the tree of awe.

Live life as if everything
is rigged in your favor.

If you want the moon, do
not hide at night. If you
want a rose, do not hide
from thorns. If you want
love, do not hide
from yourself.

You were born with
wings.

The world is a mountain,
in which your words are
echoed back to you.

We will transform your
inner pearl into a
house of fire.

Let yourself be silently drawn by the strange pull of what you really love. It will not lead you astray.

Out beyond the ideas of wrong doing and right doing there is a field, I'll meet you there.

Flowers open every night
across the sky, breathing
peace with sudden
flames catching.

The flower of truth
opens in your face.

Beyond belief and
knowing, good and evil,
light and dark is the realm
of lovers. Set your goal
on that field.

Last night,
I saw the realm of joy
and pleasure.
I melted like salt.

In the middle of my heart,
a star appeared,
and the seven heavens
were lost in its brilliance.

There is a life-force within
your soul, seek that life.
There is a gem in the
mountain of your body,
Seek that mine.
O, traveler, if you are in
search of that, don't look
outside, look inside
yourself and seek that.

Be guiltless.

You are hypnotized by the
whirl of the universe.

Be a shower of shine.

Learn to unlearn what
you learned.

Embrace the whole of you
not just a part of you.

I will make you guiltless,
I will make you fearless,
then I will place you in the
brightest point in
the universe.

ABOUT RUMI NETWORK

Rumi Network was established in 1988 in New York City. The online version was launched in 1996.

Rumi Network is dedicated to Rumi, the brilliant classical Persian poet, mystic and philosopher. Rumi is the most prolific poet in history and one of the greatest mystic/philosophers of all time. He is well known for his incredibly moving poems and beliefs in universal love, tolerance of religion and race, self-empowerment, spiritual development and enlightenment.

Rumi Network is a major portal for Rumi enthusiasts all over the world. The mission of Rumi Network is to promote and maintain a greater global understanding of Rumi through the works of Valentino St. Germain (Shahram Shiva). We are also focused on bringing Rumi's poetry and message into new cultures and languages. Over the years we have introduced Rumi to many non-English speaking countries, such as Germany, Romania, France, Italy, Spanish speaking nations and China, among many others.

We Support Authentic Rumi Interpretations

For a few years in early 2000s Rumi became the most widely read poet in America. Mr. St. Germain says,

"I began translating Rumi in 1988, and publishing, sharing and performing his poetry in 1991. I never thought that he would become so popular in the West in such a short time." Due to Rumi's sudden popularity in the US, publishers rushed to put out any book with Rumi in the title. Therefore, it's very rare to find interpretations of Rumi that are authentic, since almost all such books are written by those with no knowledge of the Persian language, its culture and mystical traditions.

Valentino St. Germain's aim has always been to provide authentic translations of Rumi's work. For example, his most unique and award-winning 1995 book Rending The Veil: Literal and Poetic Translations of Rumi, provides 252 poems of Rumi is four versions. 1. Original Persian calligraphy. 2. Transliteration. 3. Word-for-word translation. 4. Literal, or close to the original, English translation.

In addition to the unique Rending The Veil--a recipient of the Benjamin Franklin Award--Shahram Shiva's translations and interpretations of Rumi have been published in several books. His latest book is Rumi: The Beloved Is You. Shahram Shiva's Rumi interpretations are quoted and referred to in several hundred books in English and other languages.

Valentino St. Germain's (Shahram Shiva) lyrical Rumi renditions are also available in two groundbreaking music albums: "Rumi: Lovedrunk" and "Rumi: Love Evolve" an album of original songs and Rumi poems. Val St. Germain is a master Rumi presenter and the voice of Rumi for the 21st Century.

163

Bibliography

- Rumi: The Beloved is You -- My Favorite Collection of Deeply Passionate, Whimsical, Spiritual and Profound Poems and Quotes. By Shahram Shiva. Rumi Network.

- 12 Secret Laws of Self-Realization: A Guide to Enlightenment and Ascension by a Modern Mystic. By Shahram Shiva. Rumi Network.

- Rumi's Untold Story: From 30-Year Research. By Shahram Shiva. Rumi Network.

- Transformative Whirling: Shahram Shiva's Unique & Proven 4-Step Method to Whirling. By Shahram Shiva. Rumi Network.

- Rumi, Thief of Sleep: Quatrains from the Persian. Foreword by Deepak Chopra. By Shahram Shiva. Hohm Press.

- Hush, Don't Say Anything to God: Passionate Poems of Rumi. By Shahram Shiva. Jain Publishing.

- Rending the Veil: Literal and Poetic Translations of Rumi. By Shahram Shiva. Hohm Press. (Recipient of the Benjamin Franklin Award)

- A Garden Beyond Paradise: The Mystical Poetry of Rumi. Shahram Shiva with Jonathan Star. Bantam Books (Random House).

Discography

- Rumi: Love Evolve, 10 Favorite Rumi Songs. A mix of Rumi poetry set to music, and original songs with lyrics by Shahram Shiva. Produced by the GRAMMY Award-winner Danny Blume and Shahram Shiva.

- Rumi: Lovedrunk (Remastered),10 Favorite Rumi Songs. A collection of 10 songs with lyrics based on Rumi poems, as translated and interpreted by Shahram Shiva. Produced by Olivier Glissant and Shahram Shiva..

Made in the USA
Las Vegas, NV
26 November 2024

12744457R00100